# SUPER PEGASUS
# SPORTS STARS

www.pegasusforkids.com

© **B. Jain Publishers (P) Ltd.** All rights reserved. No part of this book may be reproduced, stored in a retrieval system or transmitted, in any form or by any means, mechanical, photocopying, recording or otherwise, without any prior written permission of the publisher.

Published by Kuldeep Jain for B. Jain Publishers (P) Ltd., D-157, Sector 63, Noida - 201307, U.P

Printed in India

All Images © Copyright Getty Images India

# Contents

| | |
|---|---|
| 4 | Dhanraj Pillay |
| 6 | Lance Armstrong |
| 10 | Lebron James |
| 16 | Lewis Hamilton |
| 20 | Ma Long |
| 22 | Michael Phelps |
| 26 | Roger Federer |
| 30 | Sania Mirza |
| 36 | Saina Nehwal |
| 40 | Tiger Woods |
| 44 | Usain Bolt |

# Dhanraj Pillay

Dhanraj Pillay is one of the best Indian hockey players and former captain of the Indian hockey team. He is at present the manager of the Indian hockey team and plans to set up a hockey academy in Mumbai, India.

## Early Life

Pillay was born on 16 July 1968, to Nagalingam Pillay and Andalamma, in Khadki, near Pune in Maharashtra, India. Though his parents were poor, his mother encouraged her sons to play hockey. Pillay spent his youth in the Ordnance Factory staff colony where his father was a groundsman. He played there with broken hockey sticks and discarded hockey balls.

When he grew up, Pillay moved to Mumbai to be with his elder brother Ramesh, who was playing for RCF in the Mumbai League. Ramesh had already played for India in international matches and his guidance helped Dhanraj develop his skills as a speedy striker. Carvalho, the famous hockey player and coach, noticed Pillay's super-fast speed and invited him to join Mahindra & Mahindra team in Mumbai.

## International Career

Pillay played his first international match in 1989 when he represented India in the Allwyn Asia Cup in New Delhi. From that tournament, he never looked back. At the time of his retirement in 2004, he had played 339 international matches. He has scored around 170 goals in his career. He is the only player to have played in four Olympics (1992, 1996, 2000, and 2004), four World Cups (1990, 1994, 1998, and 2002), four Champions Trophies (1995, 1996, 2002, and 2003), and four Asian Games (1990, 1994, 1998, and 2002). While he was captain of the Indian Hockey team, India won the Asian Games (1998) and Asia Cup (2003). Pillay was also the highest goal scorer in the Bangkok Asian Games and was the only Indian player to figure in the World Eleven side during the 1994 World Cup at Sydney.

## Club Hockey

Pillay has played for foreign clubs like the Indian Gymkhana (London), HC Lyon (France), BSN HC & Telekom Malaysia HC (Malaysia), Abahani Limited (Dhaka), HTC Stuttgart Kickers (Germany) and Khalsa Sports Club (Hong Kong). He has also played in the Premier Hockey League for the Maratha Warriors.

## Awards

Pillay is the recipient of India's highest sporting honour, the Rajiv Gandhi Khel Ratna award for 1999-2000. He was awarded the Padma Shri, a civilian award, in 2001. He was the winning captain of the victorious Asian Games 2002 hockey team. He was awarded the Player of the Tournament award in the 2002 Champions trophy in Germany.

## Achievements

- Highest goal scorer in the Bangkok Asian Games
- Member of World Eleven side during the 1994 World Cup
- Padma Shri (2000)
- Rajiv Gandhi Khel Ratna Award (1999)

# Lance Armstrong

Lance Armstrong is one of the greatest road racing cyclists in sports history. He has won the premier event of the sport, the Tour de France, a record seven times. He is also known for overcoming cancer and for his charitable foundation— The Lance Armstrong Foundation.

## Early Life

Born on 18 September 1971, in Plano, Texas, Armstrong was raised by his mother Linda, in the suburbs of Dallas, Texas. At a very young age of 12, Armstrong started showing his skills as an endurance athlete by standing fourth in the Texas state 1,500-meter freestyle swimming competition. Soon after, he discovered the triathlons, where you swim, bike and run. He started participating in the triathlons, and by the age of 16, he was the top ranked triathlete in the 19-and-under division. His favourite and best event was cycling, and realising that, Armstrong began to focus on it more.

Once Armstrong began to focus his efforts on cycling, he quickly became one of the top cyclists in the US and in the world. Armstrong turned professional in 1992 with the Motorola Cycling team. In 1993, he was both the US National Cycling Champion and the World Cycling

Champion. He continued to compete in races in Europe and winning awards. In 1996, he became the first American to win the Tour Dupont and La Flèche Wallonut tournaments. In 1996, he rode for the Olympic team, but stood 12th in the road race. He seemed uncharacteristically tired.

## Cancer

In October 1996, Armstrong was diagnosed with testicular cancer. Well advanced, it had spread to his brain, abdomen, lungs and lymph nodes. His chances of survival were low. Armstrong then underwent multiple surgeries along with chemotherapy. After fighting a long battle with cancer, he was declared cancer-free in February 1997. He came back to the world of cycling better than before.

### The Comeback

Three years after being diagnosed with cancer, Armstrong won the most prestigious race in his sport, the Tour de France. Before he had achieved this feat, he had only won a few stages in Tour de France. Even more amazing was the fact that he continued to win the race every year for seven years in a row. From 1999 to 2005, Armstrong dominated the world of cycling, winning every Tour de France. This was two more than any other cyclist in history.

In 2005, Armstrong announced his retirement from professional cycling. He did make a short comeback again in 2009, when he finished third in the Tour de France and in 2010, he finished 23rd. He finally retired in February 2011. In 2012, Armstrong was disqualified from all his results since August 1998, for using performance-enhancing drugs and was banned from professional cycling for life.

## The Lance Armstrong Foundation

In 1996, Armstrong formed the Lance Armstrong Foundation for Cancer, now called LiveStrong, to help people who were fighting cancer. His foundation also raises awareness about the disease. A big part of raising funds is his LiveStrong brand and store. His yellow LiveStrong wristbands are very popular and 100% of the proceeds go to helping cancer victims. One of the top 10 cancer research funds in the United States, this foundation has raised a tremendous amount of money for cancer research.

Armstrong is also associated with a non-profit organization called Athletes for Hope, along with other professional athletes. Their aim is to encourage athletes to make a difference to the world through sports philanthropy.

# Lebron James

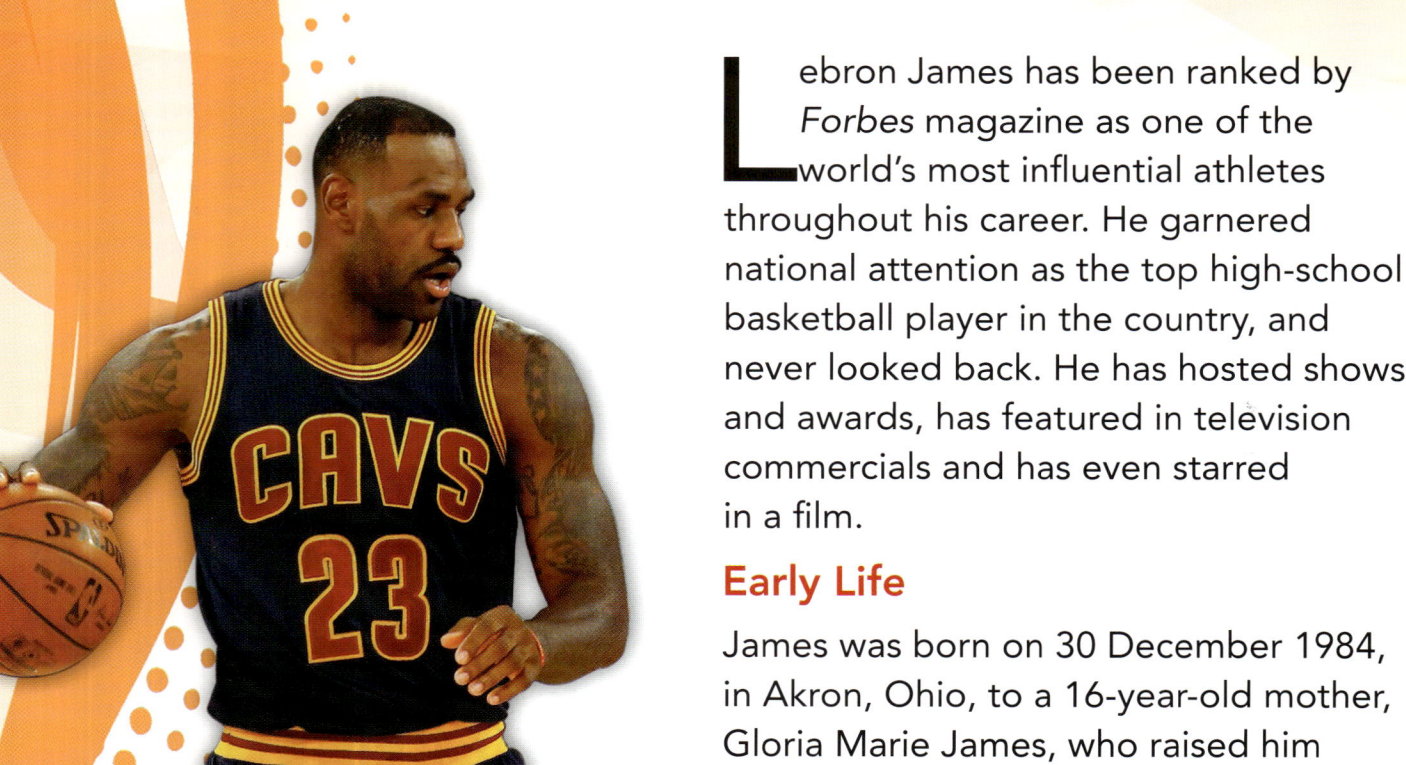

Lebron James has been ranked by *Forbes* magazine as one of the world's most influential athletes throughout his career. He garnered national attention as the top high-school basketball player in the country, and never looked back. He has hosted shows and awards, has featured in television commercials and has even starred in a film.

## Early Life

James was born on 30 December 1984, in Akron, Ohio, to a 16-year-old mother, Gloria Marie James, who raised him alone. Growing up, life was a struggle for the family, as they moved often in small neighbourhoods of Akron. During this time, his mother also struggled to find steady work. Realizing he would be better off with a more stable family environment, Gloria allowed James to move in with the family of Frank Walker, a local youth football coach, who introduced James to basketball when he was nine. In no time, Walker realized that James had a natural talent for the sport. He encouraged and refined James' talent.

As a youth, James played Amateur Athletic Union (AAU) basketball for the Northeast Ohio Shooting Stars. The team enjoyed success on a local and national level. He later attended St. Vincent-St.

Mary High School, a largely white private Catholic school.

## High School Basketball Star

James showed a natural talent for basketball at an early age. As a freshman at St. Vincent-St. Mary High School, James averaged 18 points per game. He helped the team to a Division III state title by scoring 25 points in the championship game. Word of his advanced basketball skills spread. As a high school sophomore, he was chosen for the USA Today All-USA First Team. He was the first sophomore to be selected for such an honour. His team also won the Division III state title for the second year in a row.

The following school year, James was named PARADE magazine's High School Boys Basketball Player of the Year and Gatorade Player of the Year.

James had a tremendous senior year on the court. He averaged 31.6 points per game and his team won the third straight title. The team he played for also earned the top national ranking that year. His popularity as an exceptional player increased steadily.

## With Cleveland Cavaliers

With his impressive record, it was no surprise that James was the first player to be picked in the 2003 NBA Draft. The Cleveland Cavaliers signed the powerful young forward, and he proved to be a valuable addition to the then-struggling franchise. During this time, James also signed a few endorsement deals,

including one for Nike which was worth $90 million.

During the 2003–04 season, James made history when he became the first member of the Cavalier franchise to win the NBA Rookie of the Year Award. At 20, he was the youngest player to receive the honour. Additionally, James averaged 20 points per game at that time.

During the summer of 2004, James made his Olympic debut at the Summer Games in Athens, Greece, as part of the U.S. Olympic basketball team. His talent shone at the games. He and his teammates won bronze medals at the event.

## NBA Star

James continued to excel professionally in NBA the following season. By now, he scored 27.2 points per game. He made NBA history again in 2005, when he became the youngest player to score more than 50 points in one game. He was selected for the NBA All-Star Game for the first time. He would continue to repeat this feat over the next few years.

In 2006, James helped his team defeat the Washington Wizards in the first round of playoff action. From there, the Cavaliers took on the Detroit Pistons in the Eastern Conference semifinals. James scored an average of 26.6 per game in this post season match-up, but despite his efforts his team lost. While his team wasn't at the top of rankings, James was named the Most Valuable Player in the NBA All-Star Game in 2006. The same year, James signed a new contract with the Cavaliers.

The Cavaliers proved to be stronger competitors the following season, defeating Detroit to win the Eastern Conference. In the NBA Finals against the San Antonio Spurs, however, the Cavaliers lost their championship.

During the 2007-08 season, James continued to help the Cavaliers to improve their ranking. The team lost in the semi-finals but James emerged as the rising star in NBA season.

## With Miami Heat

That summer, James travelled to Beijing, China, to play on the U.S. Olympic basketball team. The US team won by defeating Spain in the finals.

Shortly after, James announced that he would be joining the Miami Heat for the 2010-11 season. The news came as a shock to the management, fans and the Cavaliers team. Many fans accused him of betraying the Cavaliers. Nonetheless, James moved to Miami Heat. He finished second in the league during his first season with the Heat, scoring 26.7 points per game.

## Championship Wins

The 2011-12 season also saw major success for James and the Miami Heat,

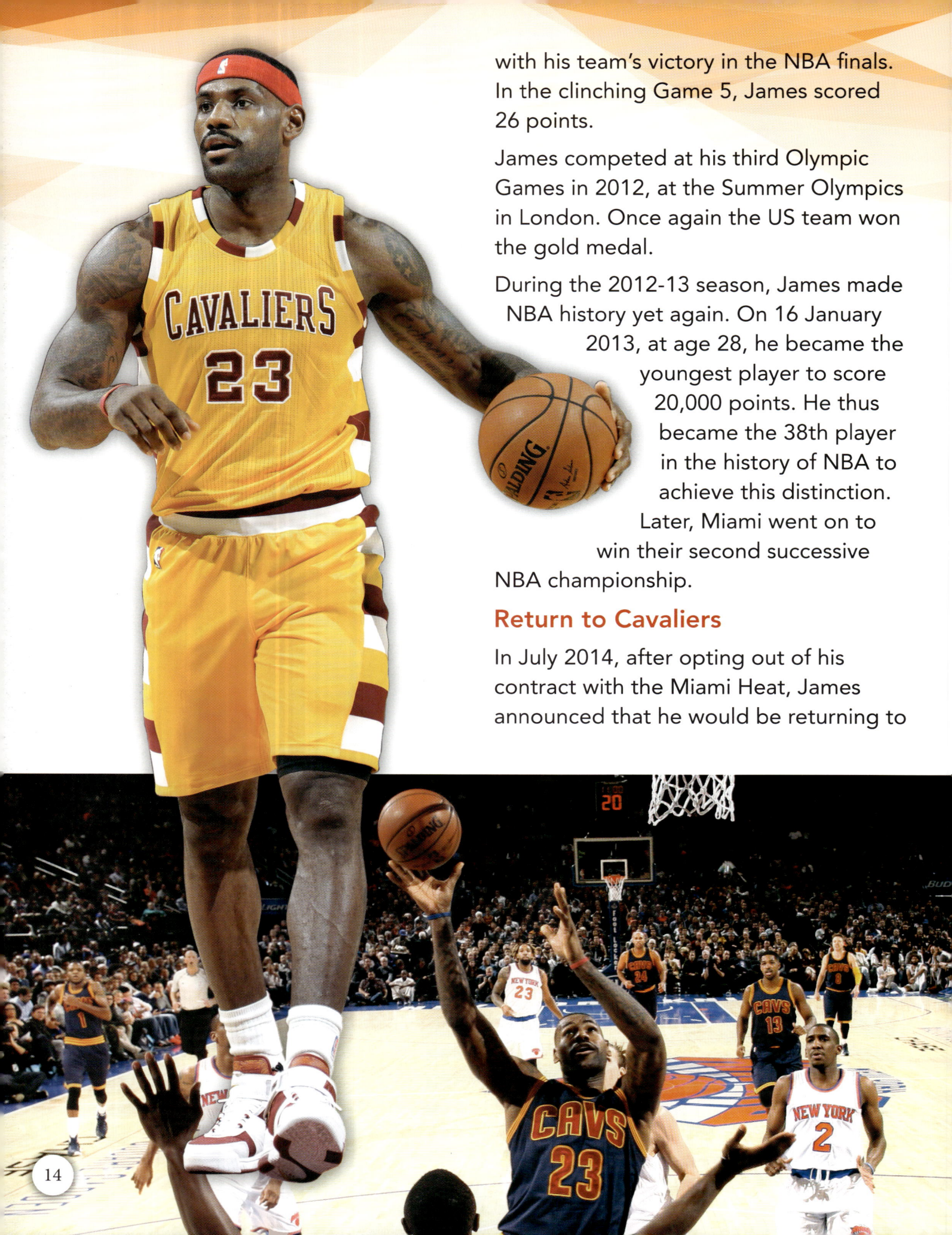

with his team's victory in the NBA finals. In the clinching Game 5, James scored 26 points.

James competed at his third Olympic Games in 2012, at the Summer Olympics in London. Once again the US team won the gold medal.

During the 2012-13 season, James made NBA history yet again. On 16 January 2013, at age 28, he became the youngest player to score 20,000 points. He thus became the 38th player in the history of NBA to achieve this distinction. Later, Miami went on to win their second successive NBA championship.

## Return to Cavaliers

In July 2014, after opting out of his contract with the Miami Heat, James announced that he would be returning to

## Personal Life

James is married to Savannah Brinson. Together they have two sons, LeBron James, Jr. and Bryce Maximus James, and one daughter, Zhuri James. He has established a charity foundation—LeBron James Family Foundation—in Akron. They have been raising money for various causes by holding bike-a-thons in Akron.

the Cavaliers. James led the Cavaliers to the NBA Finals, becoming the first player in nearly 50 years to reach the championship round in five consecutive seasons. However, due to injuries to their key players, the Cavaliers lost the championship.

# Lewis Hamilton

Lewis Hamilton is one of the youngest F1 champions in the history of Formula One racing. He is the only driver to have won at least one race in every season he has competed in.

## Early Life

Hamilton was born on 7 January 1985, to Carmen Larbalestier and Anthony Hamilton, in Stevenage, Hertfordshire, England. His parents separated when he was two and he went to live with his mother and two half-sisters. When Hamilton was six, his father bought him a radio-controlled car. Hamilton senior told him that as long as he did well at school, he would support his son's passion for racing.

## Karting Champ

Hamilton started go-karting in 1990, aged eight years, while studying at school. By the age of 10, he had won his first British Karting Championship and had already met Ron Dennis, his future boss. He had also cheekily told him that he would drive one of his F1 cars. Eventually, he kept up to his word. Between 1998 and 2000, with the backing of Dennis, Hamilton won both the European and World Karting titles. In 2000, aged 15, Hamilton was crowned Karting World Number One and he remains the youngest ever to win the tournament till date.

## Dream Come True

He attended sixth-form at Cambridge Arts and Sciences before racing in the British Formula Renault Winter Series in 2001. He finished fifth overall though he had crashed in his fifth race. Seeing his technique and skill, Michael Schumacher greatly praised him. In 2002, Hamilton participated in the Formula Renault 2000 UK series with Manor Motorsport. He finished third with three wins. He stayed with Manor for another year and won the championship in 2003. The same year, he made his debut in Formula Three and went on to participate in the Macau Grand Prix and Korea Grand Prix in 2004.

Hamilton continued to race in the Formula Three races. At the end of the 2005 season, he had won 15 out of the 20 rounds. *Autosport* had also ranked him number 24 in its list of Top 200 Drivers.

In 2006, he moved to ASM's sister GP2 team ART Grand Prix, the leading team of the series. He won the championship, defeating defending champion F1 Racer Timo Glock. He went on to register considerable wins. In November 2006, Hamilton joined Fernando Alonso's team, who was impressed by his technique. Hamilton was now a Formula One driver and had accomplished his dream.

## Formula One Driver

Hamilton's first race as a Formula One driver was at the Australian Grand prix in 2007. He qualified fourth and finished third. It was then that the press realized that Hamilton was a champion in the making.

He finished in the top five in his first five races and won his first Grand Prix in Canada followed by another win in America. Later, he participated in the British Grand Prix, and finished third, but the race was memorable for him because his home crowd was 100 per cent behind him. Frustratingly, in Brazil, in the last race of the season, he finished seventh and missed out on the World Championship by merely one single point!

Then, in 2008, he comfortably won Australian Grand Prix. However, Ferrari soon became McLaren's rivals. Hamilton showed a disappointing display in Malaysia, Bahrain, Spain and Turkey. That was until Monaco 2008, where he crossed the line first. He then went on to win the British Grand Prix, the Shanghai round and, despite coming in fifth in Brazil, in the final race of the season, Hamilton got the World Championship, based on points at the age of 23. He was lauded as a champion.

The year 2009 was a disappointing one

for Hamilton as he won only two races. The next year was a more successful season as Hamilton finished second in the World Championship behind Sebastian Vettel.

In 2011, Hamilton had another disappointing racing season as he finished fifth in the World Championship rankings. Hamilton won the Canadian Grand Prix for the third time and again won the Hungarian Grand Prix. His final win of the season was in Texas where he finished fourth.

In 2013, Hamilton signed a three-year contract with Mercedes Benz. He secured his first win with his new team in Hungary, making him the first British racing driver to win in Mercedes since 1955. He has had considerable wins since then and has finished with top ranks. Today, Hamilton is among the top ranked Formula One racing drivers with many more races to win.

## Trivia

- At the age of 5, Hamilton took up Karate classes to defend himself against bullies.
- Hamilton was an avid footballer and cricketer. He is an Arsenal fan.
- He was awarded an MBE by the Queen in 2009.
- He is often called the 'first Black driver' in F1, though he is technically of mixed origin.
- In 2007, Hamilton drove at 122 mph on a French motorway and was consequently suspended from driving in the country for a month.

# Ma Long

Ma Long was 5 years old when he started learning how to play table tennis. He quickly showed his great skills at playing the game. When he was eight years old, he came to Beijing to begin his formal and more advanced training in the sport.

In 2003, Long became a part of the Chinese National Team. No sooner had he turned professional that his first world singles title came in 2004, when he won the World Junior Championship. Later, as an 18 year old, Long became the youngest world champion in 2006.

## Playing Style

Long is arguably the best table tennis player in history. His serves though appear to be regular, are extremely deceptive visually. He plays a forehand-oriented style and uses his backhand to block incoming loops. He is also the most prominent employer of the chop block, which he uses to counter slow loops.

## Career

Given his exceptional skill, Long has won both the Asian and World Junior Championships. He was the youngest world champion after winning the 2006 Bremen World Team Championship. Before turning 22, Long had huge success in singles as he reached the finals of 11 ITTF World Tour tournaments. Despite being the best tennis player in the world, Long could not participate in the 2012 Olympics due to his temporary dip in the ratings. The year 2013 was a good one for Long, when he won the China Open, the Asian Championships for the third time and the China National Games. In March 2014, Long won the Asian Cup for the fourth time. At the 2014 WTTC, he was awarded the tournament's Best Player award. He next won the China Open.

In 2015, he won the Kuwait Open and the German Open. However, his biggest win came at the 2015 WTTC. He later won the China Open for a record sixth time. In September, he won the Chinese Super League championship and in October, the World Cup in Halmstad. Known for his superb skills in table tennis, Long has presented himself as a rather tough opponent to beat.

## Fast Facts

| | |
|---|---|
| Born: | Oct. 20, 1988 |
| Place of Birth: | Liaoning, China |
| Height: | 1.75m |
| Team: | Zhejiang Ningbo Haitian |

# Michael Phelps

Swimmer Michael Phelps is one of the greatest Olympic athletes of all time. He has won 18 gold medals in his career and is the most decorated Olympian with a total of 22 medals.

## Early Life

Phelps was born on 30 June 1985, in Baltimore, Maryland. Phelps had Attention Deficit Hyperactivity Disorder (ADHD) as a child. His father Fred, an all-around athlete, was a state trooper while his mother Debbie was a middle-school principal. Later, when his parents divorced, he lived with his mother and sisters. His parents got him into swimming as a way for him to burn off some energy. At age 7, Phelps was

still a little scared to put his head under water, so his instructors allowed him to float around on his back. Soon, he started enjoying it.

Phelps did well at swimming from the start itself and was breaking records by the age of 10. In 1996, after seeing the Summer Games in Atlanta, Phelps started dreaming of becoming a champion. He started his swimming career at Loyola High School. Coach Bob Bowman saw that young Phelps had a lot of potential and skill, and that he could be a champion. Under his guidance, Phelps started his intense training to be a swimmer. By 1999, with Bowman's guidance and his own skills, Phelps made it to the U.S. National B Team.

And at the age of 15, Phelps became the youngest American male swimmer to compete at Olympic Games in 68 years. Though he did not win any medal, he was seen as a major force in competitive swimming.

## Setting World Records

In the spring of 2001, Phelps set the world record in the 200-meter butterfly, becoming the youngest male swimmer in history to set a world swimming record. Phelps was only 15 years of age at that time. He went on to break his own record in 2001 World Championships in Fukuoka, Japan. This achievement earned him his first international medal.

At the 2002 U.S. Summer Nationals, he established a new world record for the 400-meter individual medley, and U.S. records in the 100-meter butterfly and the 200-meter individual medley. At the same event, next year, he went on to break his own record in the 400-meter individual medley.

Shortly after graduating from Towson in 2003, 17-year-old Phelps set five world records, including the 200-meter individual medley at the World Championships in Barcelona, Spain. Later, during the U.S. trials for the 2004 Summer Olympics, he went on to break his own record in 400 meter individual medley. At the 2004 Olympic Games in Athens, Greece, Phelps was simply unstoppable. He went on to win eight medals including six gold. The two events in Athens, in which Phelps took bronze medals, were 200-meter freestyle and the 4-by-100-meter freestyle relay.

It was, however, at the 2008 Olympic games in Beijing, China, that Phelps made history. He won eight gold medals, the most by any athlete at the Olympics! His performance was simply phenomenal. He now had 14 Olympic gold medals, the most gold medals won by any Olympian.

In 2012, during the London Olympics, Phelps' Olympic medal count increased to 22, setting a new record for most Olympic medals. This time, he had won four gold medals and two silver ones. During the event, he also announced that he was retiring from competitive swimming. However, in mid 2013, he hinted that he may return. The stellar swimmer would not rule out a possible Olympic bid for the 2016 Summer Olympics in Rio de Janeiro. However, in April 2014, Phelps put the rumours to

rest and announced he was coming out of retirement with plans to compete at the Mesa Grand Prix in Arizona. While he did compete at the Grand Prix, Phelps made a more impressive showing at the Pan Pacific Championships held that summer in Australia by winning three gold and two silver medals.

What future records Phelps is about to set, is something everyone will have to wait for!

## Trivia

- Phelps' feet have been referred to as "fins" by the media, because he wears size 14 shoes. He has double-jointed knees and elbows, which help him deliver his famous dolphin-like kick in the water.
- Phelps swims about five hours per day and eats up to 10,000 calories in a day.
- He has a street named after him in his hometown Towson, Maryland.

# Roger Federer

Roger Federer is widely regarded as the best tennis player of the 2000s and perhaps the best tennis player of all time. Unlike many players who specialize in a particular surface (like clay, grass or hard court) or are experts in serving or maybe volleying, Federer is an all-around player. He has won major titles on all surfaces, can serve and volley and can trade ground strokes with the best. His all-around expertise and excellence in all aspects of the game is what has made him so consistently great.

## Early Life

Federer took an interest in sports at an early age, playing tennis and soccer at the age of 8. By age 11, he was among the top 3 junior tennis players in Switzerland. At age 12, he decided to focus all his attention towards playing tennis, which he felt he naturally excelled at. By 14, he was fully immersed in the game, playing two or three tournaments per month and practising rigorously.

At age 14, Federer became the national junior champion in Switzerland, and was chosen to train at the Swiss National Tennis Center in Ecublens. He joined the International Tennis Federation's junior tennis circuit in July 1996 and by 16 years of age, he had his first sponsorship. In 1998, he went on to win the Junior Wimbledon title and the Orange Bowl. The same year, he turned professional and was recognized as the ITF World Junior Tennis champion of the year.

## Tennis Star

After his entry into professional tennis, Federer became a sensation in 2001. It was because during Wimbledon that year, he knocked out the reigning singles champion Pete Sampras in the fourth round. In 2003, Federer became the first Swiss to win the coveted Wimbledon title.

At the beginning of 2004, Federer was ranked No. 2 in the world. The same year, he won the Australian Open, the U.S. Open, the ATP Masters and also retained his Wimbledon singles title. The following year, he won the Wimbledon and the U.S. Open.

Federer held on to his No. 1 ranking from 2004 into 2008. In 2006 and 2007, he won the Australian Open, Wimbledon and the U.S. Open. He was also named Laureus World Sportsman of the Year from 2005-08. In 2008, Federer had a difficult year as he only managed to win his fifth U.S. Open title. In the rest of the

competitions, he struggled. It was also first time in four years that his ranking had dropped to No. 2.

The 2009 season was a memorable one for the Swiss star. He won the French Open and was ranked among the few players who had managed to win all the four grand slams. The same year, he also defeated Andy Roddick in an epic Wimbledon final to surpass Pete Sampras' record of 15 Grand Slam singles title. Although Federer lost the U.S. Open but his brilliant all-around play led him to regain the world's No. 1 ranking. Then in 2012, he won his seventh Wimbledon title.

In the years to follow, Federer has been struggling, and his fans are waiting for the Swiss star to shine once again.

# Personal Life

In 2003, Federer established the Roger Federer Foundation, which helps provide grants to poor countries that have child mortality rates of more than 15 percent, for education and sports-related projects.

In 2009, Federer married Mirka Vavrinec, a former professional tennis player. That July, the couple became parents of identical twin girls, Myla and Charlene. On 6 May 2014, the couple welcomed their second set of twins, boys Leo and Lenny. Federer lives with his family in Bottmingen, Switzerland.

# Sania Mirza

Sania Mirza is an Indian professional tennis player, currently ranked No. 1 in the women's doubles rankings. She is one of the highest paid athletes in the country. *Time* magazine named her as one of the 50 heroes of Asia, in October 2005.

## Early Life

Sania was born on 15 November 1986, in Mumbai, Maharashtra, India, to Imran Mirza, a builder, and his wife Naseema, who worked in a printing business. Shortly after her birth, her family moved to Hyderabad where she and her younger sister, Anam, were raised in a traditional environment. Sania took up tennis at the age of six. She has been coached by her father and also Roger Anderson.

Sania attended Nasr School in Hyderabad and later graduated from St. Mary's College. She is also an excellent good swimmer.

## ITF Circuits

Sania turned professional in 2003. She won 10 singles and 13 doubles titles as a junior player. She won the 2003 Wimbledon Championships Girls' Doubles title, partnering Alisa Kleybanova. She also reached the semifinals of the 2003 US Open Girls' Doubles and the quarterfinals of the 2002 US Open Girls' Doubles.

In the senior circuit, Sania started to show

early success as she made her debut in April 2001 on the ITF Circuit as a 15-year-old. As the 2002 season began, she turned around a season of early losses to winning three straight titles.

In February 2003, Sania was given a wildcard to play in her first ever WTA tournament, at the AP Tourism Hyderabad Open. She, however, made an early exit. She had a good result representing India at the Fed Cup. She helped India win a bronze medal in the mixed doubles event of the 2002 Asian Games in Busan. Sania also picked up four gold medals at the 2003 Afro-Asian Games in Hyderabad.

## WTA Circuit and Grand Slam Tournaments

At the 2004 AP Tourism Hyderabad Open, Sania, a wildcard entrant, went on to win the doubles title with Liezel Huber. She won six ITF singles titles in 2004. Going into the 2005 Australian Open, Sania reached the third round. In February 2005, she became the first Indian woman to win a WTA title, the AP Tourism Hyderabad Open. Her good form continued at the 2005 Dubai Tennis Championships.

The same year, she reached the fourth round of the US Open. The year 2005 proved to be a good one for the young budding star in Indian tennis. She was even named as the WTA Newcomer of the Year.

Sania entered the 2006 Australian Open as a seeded player. Her efforts began to show and at the 2007 US Open, she was ranked 27. In 2007, she went on to win four doubles titles at major tournaments.

## Grand Slam Mixed Doubles Championship

Sania's ranking continued to rise and she

reached the quarterfinals at Hobart as No. 6 seed. Though she lost the tournament, she had a better show in the doubles category at the Australian Open.

In 2008, Sania represented India at the 2008 Summer Olympics in Beijing. Due to her injuries, she was eliminated early on in the tournament. Her injuries to the wrist continued to plague her all the year round. Next, at the 2009 Australian Open, in mixed doubles Sania picked up her first Grand Slam title with Mahesh Bhupathi.

She then entered the Pattaya Women's Open Tournament in Bangkok, where she reached the finals. The year 2010 was low key.

## Doubles Specialisation

Though the year 2011 started on a poor note for her, at the Premier Mandatory events in March, Sania won the doubles title. She then went on to participate at the Premier-level Family Circle Cup in Charleston. In singles, she made her first Premier quarterfinal since August 2007. In doubles, Sania won the title with Vesnina. This was her second doubles win in that season.

Later, at the 2011 French Open, Sania came up as the runner-up in the doubles finals. Next, playing at the All England Lawn Tennis Club, she came up with her personal best performance by reaching her first semi final at the Championships. Later, she went on to win the title in doubles in D.C. Going into the Australian Open, Sania reached her third grand slam semi final, partnering Elena Vesnina. While playing in the mixed doubles with Mahesh Bhupathi, she reached the semi final.

Sania played well in the next few tournaments. She then participated in the French Open in the Women's doubles (with Mattek-Sands) and the French Open mixed doubles (with Bhupathi). She won the French Open mixed doubles title with Mahesh Bhupathi.

### Top 5 Doubles Breakthrough

Sania began 2014 playing with Cara Black in the 2014 Australian Open. Seeded sixth, Sania and Cara reached the quarterfinals of the Women's Doubles.

They recorded three consecutive quarterfinal finishes in the subsequent clay tournaments. In the 2014 US Open, the pair lost in the semi finals. Sania played the mixed doubles in the 2014 US Open pairing with Bruno Soares and became the 2014 US Open Mixed Doubles Champions. She won a gold and bronze at the 17th Asian Games in Incheon, South Korea.

### Number 1 WTA Doubles Ranking

Sania began her 2015 season ranked No. 6 in the doubles

rankings. She started a new partnership with then world No. 5 Hsieh Su-wei from Taipei, China. The pair reached the semi finals of 2015 Brisbane International as the top seeds.

Sania then paired up with Swiss legend Martina Hingis. The pair entered Indian Wells as the top seeds and went on to win the title. They also won the Miami Masters event. The duo then also won the 2015 Miami Open. Sania and Martina won 2015 Family Circle Cup's double title in April 2015. With this title, Sania became the first Indian to be ranked world No. 1 in WTA's doubles rankings.

Later, the pair lost in the quarterfinals of 2015 French Open. However, they won the 2015 Wimbledon Women's double title. They also won the US Open title.

## Playing Style

Sania Mirza is an offensive baseliner with very powerful groundstroke and is known for setting up good attacks with the sheer velocity of her groundstrokes. Her main strength is her forehand, as well as her good volleying skills. She is also a great returner of serve.

## Personal Life

In April 2010, Sania Mirza married Pakistani cricketer Shoaib Malik in Hyderabad. Sania was appointed as *UN Women Goodwill Ambassador for South Asia*, in 2013, and is the first South-Asian woman to be appointed thus.

Sania has also established a tennis academy in Hyderabad. She is currently the brand ambassador for the Indian state of Telangana.

## Awards

Arjuna Award (2004)

WTA New Comer of the Year (2005)

Padma Shri (2006)

Rajiv Gandhi Khel Ratna (2015)

Padma Bhushan (2016)

# Saina Nehwal

Saina Nehwal is currently ranked No. 1 in the world by the Badminton World Federation and is the first Indian woman to achieve this feat. She is also the first Indian to win the World Junior Badminton Championship and a medal in badminton at the Olympics.

## Early Life

Saina, second daughter of Harvir Singh and Usha Rani, was born on 17 March 1990, in Hisar, Haryana, India. Her father worked as an agricultural scientist in CCS Haryana Agricultural University, Hisar, and Saina completed her first few years of schooling at the campus school there. The family later shifted to Hyderabad, where Saina completed her studies.

## Career Path

In 2006, Saina became the under-19 national champion and created history by winning the prestigious Asian Satellite Badminton tournament twice. She was the first player to do so. In May 2006, the 16-year-old Saina also became the first Indian woman and the youngest player from Asia to win the Philippines Open. The same year Saina was also the runner-up at the 2006 BWF World Junior Championships, where she lost a hard fought match to the Chinese top seed. In 2008, she became the first Indian to win the World Junior Badminton Championships.

She became the first Indian woman to reach the quarterfinals at the Olympic Games by upsetting the top seed in a thrilling match. In September 2008, she won the Yonex Chinese Taipei Open 2008 and was named 'The Most Promising Player'.

## Super Winner

On 21 June 2009, she became the first Indian to win a BWF Super Series title. She had thus won the most prominent badminton series in the world by winning the Indonesia Open. In August 2009, she reached the quarterfinals of world championship, which she lost.

Saina successfully led the Indian Women Team to the quarterfinal stage of the 2010 Uber Cup finals. She became the first Indian woman to reach the semifinals of 2010 All-England Super Series where she lost.

She won the second Super Series title of her career by winning the Singapore Open. With this win, Saina reached a career high of world no. 3 in the women's singles badminton world rankings on 24 June 2010. Saina defended her Indonesia Open super series title in three tough games and went on to win her third Super

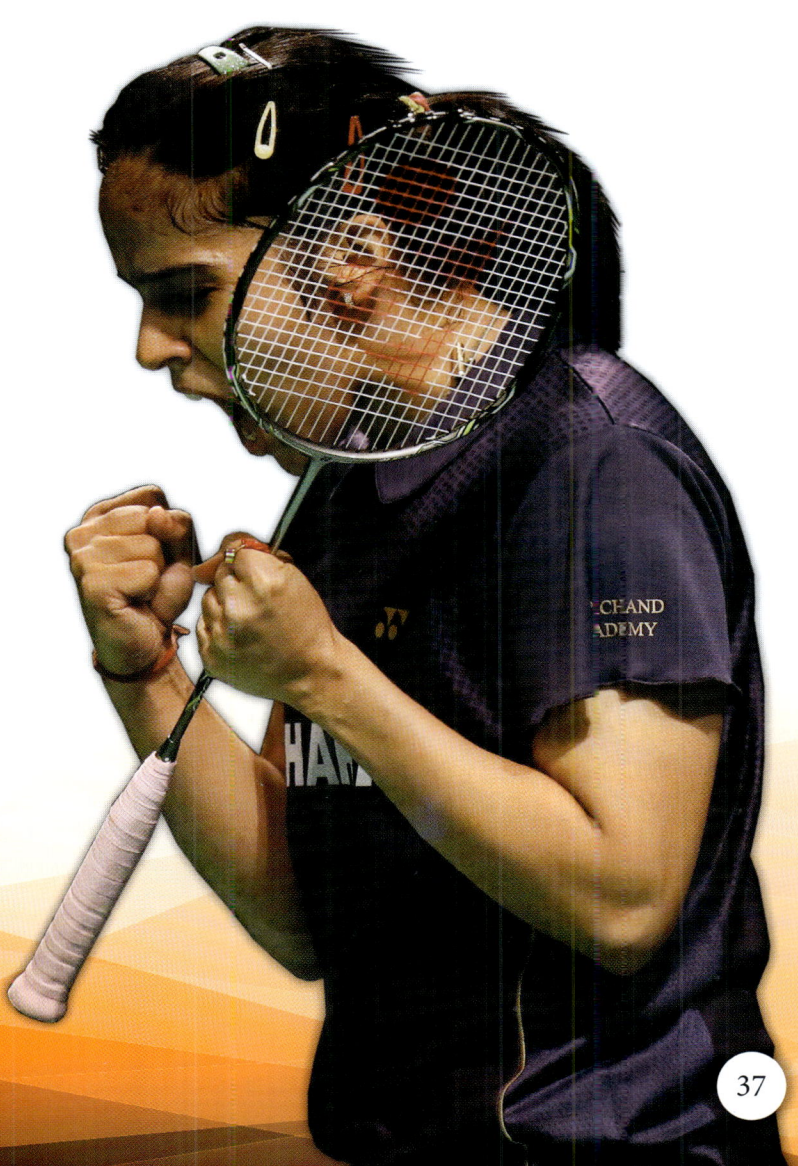

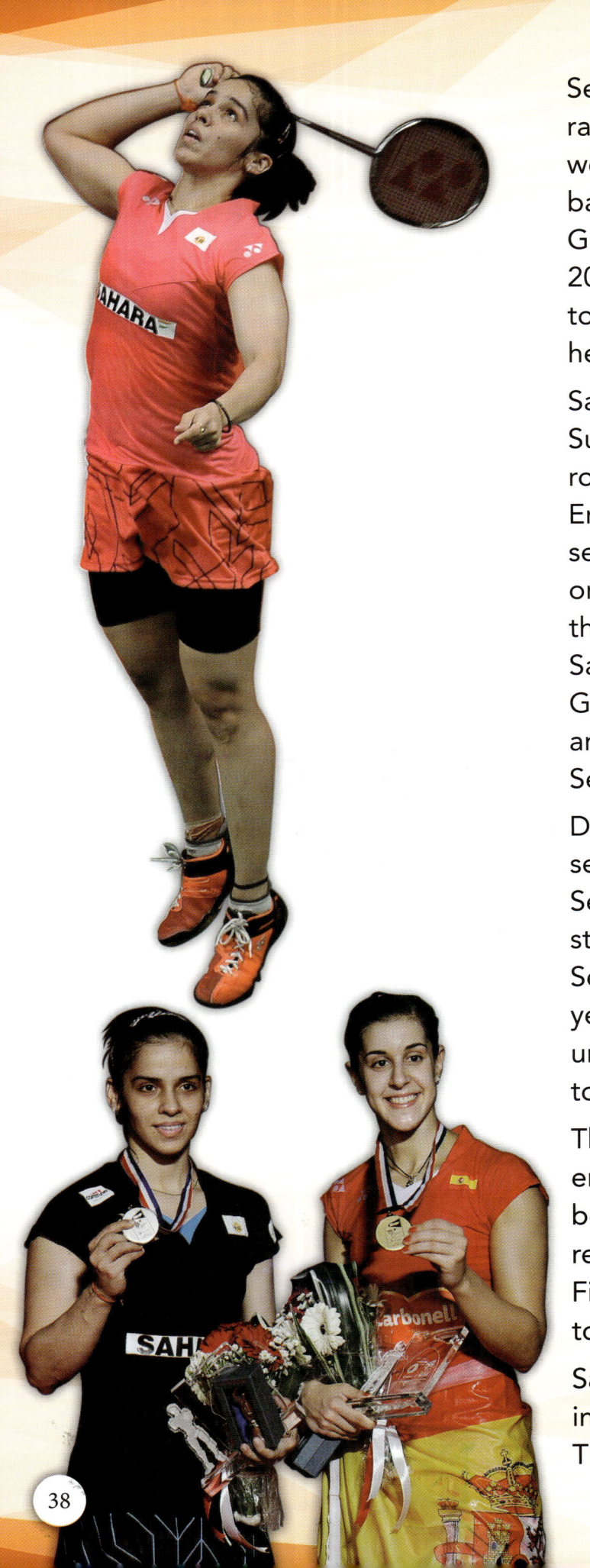

Series title. After this tournament she was ranked No. 2 in the world. Top seed Saina, won the gold medal in the Women's Singles badminton event in the 2010 Commonwealth Games held in New Delhi. In December 2010, she participated in the last Super Series tournament of the year and went on to win her fourth career Super Series title.

Saina crashed out of the 2011 Korea Open Super Series Premier in January in the early rounds. She went on to lose in the 2011 All England Super Series Premier. This was her second early exit of the year. She later went on to win the Wilson Badminton Swiss Open, thus breaking her losing streak. Second seed Saina then went on to win the Swiss Open Grand Prix Gold badminton title. She posed an early exit from the Indian Open Super Series in Delhi.

Defending champion Saina lost in the second round of Singapore Open Super Series. Saina, in her attempt to record a third straight win at the Indonesia Open Super Series Premier, reached the finals, but lost yet again. Throughout that season, she was unable to manage a win, losing the tournaments at various stages.

The tables turned for her during the season-ending tournament in December. She became the first Indian singles player to reach the final of BWF Super Series Masters Finals. Though she lost the final, it was a tough match and lasted over an hour.

Saina successfully won her Swiss Open Title in March 2012. In June 2012, she lifted the Thailand Open Grand Prix Gold title. She

next went on to win the Indonesia Open Super Series. It was her third Indonesia Open title. In August at the London Olympics, she went to win a bronze medal. Later in October she won the Denmark Open Super Series Premier.

On 26 January 2014, Saina defeated World Championship bronze medalist P.V. Sindhu to win the Women's Singles of India Open Grand Prix Gold tournament. In March 2014, world no. 4 Saina crashed out of the 2014 All England Super Series Premier in the quarterfinals. In June, she lifted the trophy, winning the Women's Singles of 2014 Australian Super Series. This win boosted her ranking to No. 7. She later became the first Indian woman to win the China Open Super Series Premier.

Defending champion Saina won the 2015 India Open Grand Prix Gold. She later became the first Indian woman to reach the finals of All England Open Badminton Championships which she lost. On 29 March 2015, Saina won her maiden women's singles title at the India Open BWF Super Series. The champion continues to shine.

## Awards

Arjuna Award (2009)

Rajiv Gandhi Khel Ratna (2009-2010)

Padma Shri (2010)

# Tiger Woods

Athlete Eldrick Tont Woods, better known as Tiger Woods, is the only child of an African-American Army officer father and a Thai mother. He was born on 30 December 1975, in Cypress, California. When Woods was a child, his father began calling him "Tiger" in honour of a fellow soldier and friend who had the same name. When Tiger was a mere child, he learned to play golf. His father, Earl, served as his teacher and mentor.

## A Prodigy

At age 3, Tiger had shot a 48 over nine holes over the Cypress Naval course. Later by the age of 5, he had appeared in *Golf Digest*. Around the age of 8, Woods had become extremely proficient at the game, even showing off his skills on television shows. He went on to win Junior World Championships six times, including four consecutive wins. By 13 years of age, he had impressed some of the greatest names in the sport with his potential and skill.

Later on, Woods studied at Stanford University, and won a number of amateur U.S. golf titles before turning professional in 1996. He shot to fame after winning the U.S. Masters at Augusta in 1997, at a very young age of 21. Woods was the youngest man and the first African-

American man to win the prestigious title. In his first appearance at the British Open later that year, Woods tied the course record of 64. The next few years brought even more success, including four U.S. PGA titles, three U.S. Open wins, three Open Championship wins and three U.S. Masters wins.

In 2003, more victories followed and then in October of 2004, he married his long time girlfriend and a Swedish model, Elin Nordegren. After his marriage, he returned to playing golf and with six major tournament wins, he was voted the PGA Tour Player of Year. It was the seventh time in the past nine years that he had been awarded the title.

## Personal Life

Woods experienced a great personal loss in 2006. His father died in May after battling prostate cancer. Despite his grief, Woods returned to golf and won several events, including the PGA Championship and the British Open.

The next season was marked by many wins personally and professionally. During this time, his wife gave birth to the couple's first child.

Woods won the U.S. Open in 2008, despite the fact that he was in visible pain. It was so because he had undergone a knee surgery earlier that year. He was recovering at the time of the tournament.

His performance in this particular tournament is considered his greatest win till date. With this win, Tiger had his 14th major title win.

## Injury and Comeback

After the tournament, Woods announced that he was going to miss the remaining season in order to recover from his injuries. Later, in early 2009, Woods along with his wife Elin welcomed their second child, Charlie Axel Woods.

A few weeks later, Woods returned to the world of golf. This was the first time he was competing in a competition since his injury. However, he wasn't impressive and he fell out of the contention of the U.S. Open. Although Woods' comeback had not been as auspicious as he had hoped, he remained No. 1 in the world golf rankings. 2009 turned out to be a year without any win for Woods.

During this time, he and his wife also separated. Woods made a return to golf in April of 2010, but he was not quite at the top of his game. His first competition at the 2010 Masters Tournament in Augusta, Georgia, resulted in a fourth place finish. Soon after, he took a hiatus from golf due to a neck injury. Later, at the 2010 U.S. Open, Woods finished in a tie for fourth place.

## Second Innings

After years of turmoil, Woods finally got his golf game clicking again in 2012. He won the Arnold Palmer Invitational in March for his first PGA Tour victory since 2009. In 2013, he won five tournaments and was named the PGA Tour Player of the Year for the eleventh time.

However, just as Woods appeared primed to resume his march toward Jack Nicklaus' record of 18 major championships, injuries flared up to derail his performance. Woods underwent back surgery in March 2014, and is still struggling to return to competitive play. Wood's "roaring" comebacks at the end of tournaments are legendary. Fans and golf enthusiasts are eagerly awaiting the return of golf's brightest star.

## Trivia

Tiger Woods is the only athlete to be named *Sports Illustrated's Sportsman of the Year* twice and *Associated Press Male Athlete of the Year* four times.

He ranked 2nd on *Forbes* magazine's annual list of '100 Most Powerful Celebrities' in June 2007 and again in June 2008.

He shot a 48 over nine holes over Cypress Navy course when was just three years old.

At the age of 15, Woods became the youngest ever U.S. Junior Amateur champion (a record which stood until it was broken by Jim Liu in 2010).

# Usain Bolt

Jamaican sprinter Usain Bolt is the fastest man in the world. He is the first man to win both the 100m and 200m races at consecutive Olympic Games, as well as the first man to ever win back-to-back gold medals in double sprints. He is also the first man in history to set three world records in a single Olympic Games competition.

## Early Life

Bolt was born on 21 August 1986, in a small town Trelawny, in Jamaica to Wellesley and Jennifer Bolt. His parents ran a local grocery store. Both a standout cricket player and a sprinter early on, Bolt's natural speed was noticed by coaches at school, and he began to focus solely on sprinting and took coaching from Pablo McNeil, a former Olympic sprint athlete. At that time Bolt could think of nothing but sports. By the time he was 12, Bolt was the fastest runner in his school. Bolt is among the few athletes who have won the world championships at the youth, junior and senior levels of an athletic event. Later, Glen Mills became Bolt's coach and mentor. As early as age 14, Bolt was impressing fans of sprinting with his lightning speed, and he won his first high school championship medal in 200m race in 2001.

## Rise to Prominence

At the age of 15, Bolt took his first shot at success on the world stage at the 2002 World Junior Championships in Kingston, Jamaica. He won the 200m dash and became the youngest world-junior gold medalist ever. His popularity was growing in his home crowd. This achievement had come about when Bolt was not serious about sprinting. He continued to live like a normal teenager, eating fast food, playing basketball, and often, to his coach's dismay, playing pranks. His lifestyle lacked discipline and this worried his coach, who did not want Bolt to rely on his natural ability to beat his opponent. However, Bolt's feats had impressed the athletics world, and he received the International Association of Athletics Foundation's Rising Star Award that year and the apt nickname "Lightning Bolt."

## Professional Career

Despite a nagging hamstring injury, Bolt was chosen for the Jamaican Olympic squad for the 2004 Athens Olympics. However, he was not able to compete due to a leg injury.

It was, however, in 2007 that he proved his worth. He broke the national record held for over 30 years in 200m and earned two silver medals at the World Championship in Osaka, Japan. Only then

did Bolt decide to be a sprinter and took his ability seriously. He then began his training rigorously.

## Olympic Gold and World Records

At the Beijing Summer Olympics in 2008, Bolt represented Jamaica in the 100m and 200m racing events. In the 100-meter final, Bolt won the race and also set a new world record at 9.69 seconds. Interestingly, towards the end of the race, he had visibly slowed down to celebrate his win and also one of his shoelaces was untied! He also won the 200m race and set a world record. He thus became an athlete who had not only won the 100m and 200m races but had also set world records in both. He also won gold in 400m with his teammates. Later, Bolt said that his priority was to win the gold medal and not set a world record.

At the 2012 Summer Olympic Games, held in London, Bolt won his fourth Olympic gold medal in the men's 100m race. Bolt ran the race in 9.63 seconds, a new Olympic record. The win marked Bolt's second consecutive gold medal in the 100m event. He went on to compete in the men's 200m event, claiming his second consecutive gold medal in that race. He is the first man to win both the 100m and 200m in consecutive Olympic Games, as well as the first man to ever win back-to-back gold medals in double sprints.

## Accolades

In 2015, Bolt faced some challenges. He came in **second** at the Nassau IAAF World Relays in May, but secured an individual win in the 200m event at Ostrava Golden Spike event that same month. He also dominated the 200m race at the New York Addias Grand Prix that June.

Bolt is currently considered to be the fastest human being who is living or who has ever lived.

## Trivia

Bolt has his own clothing line in conjunction with PUMA. He also has his own watch made by Hublot. Bolt has his own headphone range 'Soul by Usain Bolt.' Bolt owns a restaurant 'Tracks & Records' in Kingston, Jamaica.
He has his own Apple app. Launched in 2012, for the users of Apple iOS phones, the 'Bolt!' game application quickly became the No. 1 application in Jamaica.

# Hall of Fame

**Dhanraj Pillay**
Hockey

**Lance Armstrong**
Cycling

**Lebron James**
Basketball

**Roger Federer**
Lawn Tennis

**Ma Long**
Table Tennis

**Lewis Hamilton**
Formula One Racing Driver

**Michael Phelps**
Swimming

**Sania Mirza**
Lawn Tennis

**Saina Nehwal**
Badminton

**Tiger Woods**
Golf

**Usain Bolt**
Racing